THANK YOU!

Eugen Diogenes

THANK YOU!

VERY MUCH!

Bibliografische Information der Deutschen Nationalbibliothek:
Die Deutsche Nationalbibliothek verzeichnet diese Publikation in der Deutschen Nationalbibliografie; detaillierte bibliografische Daten sind im Internet über http://dnb.dnb.de abrufbar.

Herstellung und Verlag: BoD — Books on Demand, Norderstedt

*ISBN: 978-3-**746014487***

THANK YOU! THANK YOU! THANK YOU! THANK YOU!

THANK YOU!   THANK YOU!   THANK YOU!   THANK YOU!

THANK YOU!   THANK YOU!   THANK YOU!   THANK YOU!

THANK YOU!   THANK YOU!   THANK YOU!   THANK YOU!

THANK YOU!   THANK YOU!   THANK YOU!   THANK YOU!

THANK YOU!   THANK YOU!   THANK YOU!   THANK YOU!

THANK YOU!   THANK YOU!   THANK YOU!   THANK YOU!

THANK YOU!   THANK YOU!   THANK YOU!   THANK YOU!

THANK YOU!   THANK YOU!   THANK YOU!   THANK YOU!

THANK YOU!   THANK YOU!   THANK YOU!   THANK YOU!

THANK YOU!   THANK YOU!   THANK YOU!   THANK YOU!

THANK YOU!   THANK YOU!   THANK YOU!   THANK YOU!

THANK YOU!   THANK YOU!   THANK YOU!   THANK YOU!

THANK YOU!   THANK YOU!   THANK YOU!   THANK YOU!

THANK YOU!   THANK YOU!   THANK YOU!   THANK YOU!

THANK YOU!   THANK YOU!   THANK YOU!   THANK YOU!

THANK YOU! THANK YOU! THANK YOU! THANK YOU!

THANK YOU!   THANK YOU!   THANK YOU!   THANK YOU!

THANK YOU!   THANK YOU!   THANK YOU!   THANK YOU!

THANK YOU!   THANK YOU!   THANK YOU!   THANK YOU!

THANK YOU!   THANK YOU!   THANK YOU!   THANK YOU!

THANK YOU!   THANK YOU!   THANK YOU!   THANK YOU!

THANK YOU!   THANK YOU!   THANK YOU!   THANK YOU!

THANK YOU!   THANK YOU!   THANK YOU!   THANK YOU!

THANK YOU!   THANK YOU!   THANK YOU!   THANK YOU!

THANK YOU!   THANK YOU!   THANK YOU!   THANK YOU!

THANK YOU!   THANK YOU!   THANK YOU!   THANK YOU!

THANK YOU!   THANK YOU!   THANK YOU!   THANK YOU!

THANK YOU!   THANK YOU!   THANK YOU!   THANK YOU!

THANK YOU!   THANK YOU!   THANK YOU!   THANK YOU!

THANK YOU!   THANK YOU!   THANK YOU!   THANK YOU!

THANK YOU!   THANK YOU!   THANK YOU!   THANK YOU!

THANK YOU! THANK YOU! THANK YOU! THANK YOU!

THANK YOU!   THANK YOU!   THANK YOU!   THANK YOU!

THANK YOU!   THANK YOU!   THANK YOU!   THANK YOU!

THANK YOU!   THANK YOU!   THANK YOU!   THANK YOU!

THANK YOU!   THANK YOU!   THANK YOU!   THANK YOU!

THANK YOU!   THANK YOU!   THANK YOU!   THANK YOU!

THANK YOU!   THANK YOU!   THANK YOU!   THANK YOU!

THANK YOU!   THANK YOU!   THANK YOU!   THANK YOU!

THANK YOU!   THANK YOU!   THANK YOU!   THANK YOU!

THANK YOU!   THANK YOU!   THANK YOU!   THANK YOU!

THANK YOU!   THANK YOU!   THANK YOU!   THANK YOU!

THANK YOU!   THANK YOU!   THANK YOU!   THANK YOU!

THANK YOU!   THANK YOU!   THANK YOU!   THANK YOU!

THANK YOU!   THANK YOU!   THANK YOU!   THANK YOU!

THANK YOU!   THANK YOU!   THANK YOU!   THANK YOU!

THANK YOU!   THANK YOU!   THANK YOU!   THANK YOU!

THANK YOU! THANK YOU! THANK YOU! THANK YOU!

THANK YOU!	THANK YOU!	THANK YOU!	THANK YOU!
THANK YOU!	THANK YOU!	THANK YOU!	THANK YOU!
THANK YOU!	THANK YOU!	THANK YOU!	THANK YOU!
THANK YOU!	THANK YOU!	THANK YOU!	THANK YOU!
THANK YOU!	THANK YOU!	THANK YOU!	THANK YOU!
THANK YOU!	THANK YOU!	THANK YOU!	THANK YOU!
THANK YOU!	THANK YOU!	THANK YOU!	THANK YOU!
THANK YOU!	THANK YOU!	THANK YOU!	THANK YOU!
THANK YOU!	THANK YOU!	THANK YOU!	THANK YOU!
THANK YOU!	THANK YOU!	THANK YOU!	THANK YOU!
THANK YOU!	THANK YOU!	THANK YOU!	THANK YOU!
THANK YOU!	THANK YOU!	THANK YOU!	THANK YOU!
THANK YOU!	THANK YOU!	THANK YOU!	THANK YOU!
THANK YOU!	THANK YOU!	THANK YOU!	THANK YOU!
THANK YOU!	THANK YOU!	THANK YOU!	THANK YOU!

THANK YOU! THANK YOU! THANK YOU! THANK YOU!

THANK YOU!	THANK YOU!	THANK YOU!	THANK YOU!
THANK YOU!	THANK YOU!	THANK YOU!	THANK YOU!
THANK YOU!	THANK YOU!	THANK YOU!	THANK YOU!
THANK YOU!	THANK YOU!	THANK YOU!	THANK YOU!
THANK YOU!	THANK YOU!	THANK YOU!	THANK YOU!
THANK YOU!	THANK YOU!	THANK YOU!	THANK YOU!
THANK YOU!	THANK YOU!	THANK YOU!	THANK YOU!
THANK YOU!	THANK YOU!	THANK YOU!	THANK YOU!
THANK YOU!	THANK YOU!	THANK YOU!	THANK YOU!
THANK YOU!	THANK YOU!	THANK YOU!	THANK YOU!
THANK YOU!	THANK YOU!	THANK YOU!	THANK YOU!
THANK YOU!	THANK YOU!	THANK YOU!	THANK YOU!
THANK YOU!	THANK YOU!	THANK YOU!	THANK YOU!
THANK YOU!	THANK YOU!	THANK YOU!	THANK YOU!
THANK YOU!	THANK YOU!	THANK YOU!	THANK YOU!
THANK YOU!	THANK YOU!	THANK YOU!	THANK YOU!

THANK YOU! THANK YOU! THANK YOU! THANK YOU!

THANK YOU! THANK YOU! THANK YOU! THANK YOU!

THANK YOU! THANK YOU! THANK YOU! THANK YOU!

THANK YOU! THANK YOU! THANK YOU! THANK YOU!

THANK YOU! THANK YOU! THANK YOU! THANK YOU!

THANK YOU! THANK YOU! THANK YOU! THANK YOU!

THANK YOU! THANK YOU! THANK YOU! THANK YOU!

THANK YOU! THANK YOU! THANK YOU! THANK YOU!

THANK YOU! THANK YOU! THANK YOU! THANK YOU!

THANK YOU! THANK YOU! THANK YOU! THANK YOU!

THANK YOU! THANK YOU! THANK YOU! THANK YOU!

THANK YOU! THANK YOU! THANK YOU! THANK YOU!

THANK YOU! THANK YOU! THANK YOU! THANK YOU!

THANK YOU! THANK YOU! THANK YOU! THANK YOU!

THANK YOU! THANK YOU! THANK YOU! THANK YOU!

THANK YOU! THANK YOU! THANK YOU! THANK YOU!

THANK YOU! THANK YOU! THANK YOU! THANK YOU!

THANK YOU!	THANK YOU!	THANK YOU!	THANK YOU!
THANK YOU!	THANK YOU!	THANK YOU!	THANK YOU!
THANK YOU!	THANK YOU!	THANK YOU!	THANK YOU!
THANK YOU!	THANK YOU!	THANK YOU!	THANK YOU!
THANK YOU!	THANK YOU!	THANK YOU!	THANK YOU!
THANK YOU!	THANK YOU!	THANK YOU!	THANK YOU!
THANK YOU!	THANK YOU!	THANK YOU!	THANK YOU!
THANK YOU!	THANK YOU!	THANK YOU!	THANK YOU!
THANK YOU!	THANK YOU!	THANK YOU!	THANK YOU!
THANK YOU!	THANK YOU!	THANK YOU!	THANK YOU!
THANK YOU!	THANK YOU!	THANK YOU!	THANK YOU!
THANK YOU!	THANK YOU!	THANK YOU!	THANK YOU!
THANK YOU!	THANK YOU!	THANK YOU!	THANK YOU!
THANK YOU!	THANK YOU!	THANK YOU!	THANK YOU!
THANK YOU!	THANK YOU!	THANK YOU!	THANK YOU!
THANK YOU!	THANK YOU!	THANK YOU!	THANK YOU!

THANK YOU! THANK YOU! THANK YOU! THANK YOU!

THANK YOU!	THANK YOU!	THANK YOU!	THANK YOU!
THANK YOU!	THANK YOU!	THANK YOU!	THANK YOU!
THANK YOU!	THANK YOU!	THANK YOU!	THANK YOU!
THANK YOU!	THANK YOU!	THANK YOU!	THANK YOU!
THANK YOU!	THANK YOU!	THANK YOU!	THANK YOU!
THANK YOU!	THANK YOU!	THANK YOU!	THANK YOU!
THANK YOU!	THANK YOU!	THANK YOU!	THANK YOU!
THANK YOU!	THANK YOU!	THANK YOU!	THANK YOU!
THANK YOU!	THANK YOU!	THANK YOU!	THANK YOU!
THANK YOU!	THANK YOU!	THANK YOU!	THANK YOU!
THANK YOU!	THANK YOU!	THANK YOU!	THANK YOU!
THANK YOU!	THANK YOU!	THANK YOU!	THANK YOU!
THANK YOU!	THANK YOU!	THANK YOU!	THANK YOU!
THANK YOU!	THANK YOU!	THANK YOU!	THANK YOU!
THANK YOU!	THANK YOU!	THANK YOU!	THANK YOU!

THANK YOU! THANK YOU! THANK YOU! THANK YOU!

THANK YOU!   THANK YOU!   THANK YOU!   THANK YOU!

THANK YOU!   THANK YOU!   THANK YOU!   THANK YOU!

THANK YOU!   THANK YOU!   THANK YOU!   THANK YOU!

THANK YOU!   THANK YOU!   THANK YOU!   THANK YOU!

THANK YOU!   THANK YOU!   THANK YOU!   THANK YOU!

THANK YOU!   THANK YOU!   THANK YOU!   THANK YOU!

THANK YOU!   THANK YOU!   THANK YOU!   THANK YOU!

THANK YOU!   THANK YOU!   THANK YOU!   THANK YOU!

THANK YOU!   THANK YOU!   THANK YOU!   THANK YOU!

THANK YOU!   THANK YOU!   THANK YOU!   THANK YOU!

THANK YOU!   THANK YOU!   THANK YOU!   THANK YOU!

THANK YOU!   THANK YOU!   THANK YOU!   THANK YOU!

THANK YOU!   THANK YOU!   THANK YOU!   THANK YOU!

THANK YOU!   THANK YOU!   THANK YOU!   THANK YOU!

THANK YOU!   THANK YOU!   THANK YOU!   THANK YOU!

THANK YOU! THANK YOU! THANK YOU! THANK YOU!

THANK YOU! THANK YOU! THANK YOU! THANK YOU!

THANK YOU! THANK YOU! THANK YOU! THANK YOU!

THANK YOU! THANK YOU! THANK YOU! THANK YOU!

THANK YOU! THANK YOU! THANK YOU! THANK YOU!

THANK YOU! THANK YOU! THANK YOU! THANK YOU!

THANK YOU! THANK YOU! THANK YOU! THANK YOU!

THANK YOU! THANK YOU! THANK YOU! THANK YOU!

THANK YOU! THANK YOU! THANK YOU! THANK YOU!

THANK YOU! THANK YOU! THANK YOU! THANK YOU!

THANK YOU! THANK YOU! THANK YOU! THANK YOU!

THANK YOU! THANK YOU! THANK YOU! THANK YOU!

THANK YOU! THANK YOU! THANK YOU! THANK YOU!

THANK YOU! THANK YOU! THANK YOU! THANK YOU!

THANK YOU! THANK YOU! THANK YOU! THANK YOU!

THANK YOU! THANK YOU! THANK YOU! THANK YOU!

THANK YOU! THANK YOU! THANK YOU! THANK YOU!

THANK YOU! THANK YOU! THANK YOU! THANK YOU!

THANK YOU! THANK YOU! THANK YOU! THANK YOU!

THANK YOU! THANK YOU! THANK YOU! THANK YOU!

THANK YOU! THANK YOU! THANK YOU! THANK YOU!

THANK YOU! THANK YOU! THANK YOU! THANK YOU!

THANK YOU! THANK YOU! THANK YOU! THANK YOU!

THANK YOU! THANK YOU! THANK YOU! THANK YOU!

THANK YOU! THANK YOU! THANK YOU! THANK YOU!

THANK YOU! THANK YOU! THANK YOU! THANK YOU!

THANK YOU! THANK YOU! THANK YOU! THANK YOU!

THANK YOU! THANK YOU! THANK YOU! THANK YOU!

THANK YOU! THANK YOU! THANK YOU! THANK YOU!

THANK YOU! THANK YOU! THANK YOU! THANK YOU!

THANK YOU! THANK YOU! THANK YOU! THANK YOU!

THANK YOU!	THANK YOU!	THANK YOU!	THANK YOU!
THANK YOU!	THANK YOU!	THANK YOU!	THANK YOU!
THANK YOU!	THANK YOU!	THANK YOU!	THANK YOU!
THANK YOU!	THANK YOU!	THANK YOU!	THANK YOU!
THANK YOU!	THANK YOU!	THANK YOU!	THANK YOU!
THANK YOU!	THANK YOU!	THANK YOU!	THANK YOU!
THANK YOU!	THANK YOU!	THANK YOU!	THANK YOU!
THANK YOU!	THANK YOU!	THANK YOU!	THANK YOU!
THANK YOU!	THANK YOU!	THANK YOU!	THANK YOU!
THANK YOU!	THANK YOU!	THANK YOU!	THANK YOU!
THANK YOU!	THANK YOU!	THANK YOU!	THANK YOU!
THANK YOU!	THANK YOU!	THANK YOU!	THANK YOU!
THANK YOU!	THANK YOU!	THANK YOU!	THANK YOU!
THANK YOU!	THANK YOU!	THANK YOU!	THANK YOU!
THANK YOU!	THANK YOU!	THANK YOU!	THANK YOU!

THANK YOU! THANK YOU! THANK YOU! THANK YOU!

THANK YOU!	THANK YOU!	THANK YOU!	THANK YOU!
THANK YOU!	THANK YOU!	THANK YOU!	THANK YOU!
THANK YOU!	THANK YOU!	THANK YOU!	THANK YOU!
THANK YOU!	THANK YOU!	THANK YOU!	THANK YOU!
THANK YOU!	THANK YOU!	THANK YOU!	THANK YOU!
THANK YOU!	THANK YOU!	THANK YOU!	THANK YOU!
THANK YOU!	THANK YOU!	THANK YOU!	THANK YOU!
THANK YOU!	THANK YOU!	THANK YOU!	THANK YOU!
THANK YOU!	THANK YOU!	THANK YOU!	THANK YOU!
THANK YOU!	THANK YOU!	THANK YOU!	THANK YOU!
THANK YOU!	THANK YOU!	THANK YOU!	THANK YOU!
THANK YOU!	THANK YOU!	THANK YOU!	THANK YOU!
THANK YOU!	THANK YOU!	THANK YOU!	THANK YOU!
THANK YOU!	THANK YOU!	THANK YOU!	THANK YOU!
THANK YOU!	THANK YOU!	THANK YOU!	THANK YOU!
THANK YOU!	THANK YOU!	THANK YOU!	THANK YOU!

THANK YOU! THANK YOU! THANK YOU! THANK YOU!

THANK YOU!	THANK YOU!	THANK YOU!	THANK YOU!
THANK YOU!	THANK YOU!	THANK YOU!	THANK YOU!
THANK YOU!	THANK YOU!	THANK YOU!	THANK YOU!
THANK YOU!	THANK YOU!	THANK YOU!	THANK YOU!
THANK YOU!	THANK YOU!	THANK YOU!	THANK YOU!
THANK YOU!	THANK YOU!	THANK YOU!	THANK YOU!
THANK YOU!	THANK YOU!	THANK YOU!	THANK YOU!
THANK YOU!	THANK YOU!	THANK YOU!	THANK YOU!
THANK YOU!	THANK YOU!	THANK YOU!	THANK YOU!
THANK YOU!	THANK YOU!	THANK YOU!	THANK YOU!
THANK YOU!	THANK YOU!	THANK YOU!	THANK YOU!
THANK YOU!	THANK YOU!	THANK YOU!	THANK YOU!
THANK YOU!	THANK YOU!	THANK YOU!	THANK YOU!
THANK YOU!	THANK YOU!	THANK YOU!	THANK YOU!
THANK YOU!	THANK YOU!	THANK YOU!	THANK YOU!

THANK YOU! THANK YOU! THANK YOU! THANK YOU!

THANK YOU! THANK YOU! THANK YOU! THANK YOU!

THANK YOU! THANK YOU! THANK YOU! THANK YOU!

THANK YOU! THANK YOU! THANK YOU! THANK YOU!

THANK YOU! THANK YOU! THANK YOU! THANK YOU!

THANK YOU! THANK YOU! THANK YOU! THANK YOU!

THANK YOU! THANK YOU! THANK YOU! THANK YOU!

THANK YOU! THANK YOU! THANK YOU! THANK YOU!

THANK YOU! THANK YOU! THANK YOU! THANK YOU!

THANK YOU! THANK YOU! THANK YOU! THANK YOU!

THANK YOU! THANK YOU! THANK YOU! THANK YOU!

THANK YOU! THANK YOU! THANK YOU! THANK YOU!

THANK YOU! THANK YOU! THANK YOU! THANK YOU!

THANK YOU! THANK YOU! THANK YOU! THANK YOU!

THANK YOU! THANK YOU! THANK YOU! THANK YOU!

THANK YOU! THANK YOU! THANK YOU! THANK YOU!

THANK YOU! THANK YOU! THANK YOU! THANK YOU!

THANK YOU!   THANK YOU!   THANK YOU!   THANK YOU!

THANK YOU!   THANK YOU!   THANK YOU!   THANK YOU!

THANK YOU!   THANK YOU!   THANK YOU!   THANK YOU!

THANK YOU!   THANK YOU!   THANK YOU!   THANK YOU!

THANK YOU!   THANK YOU!   THANK YOU!   THANK YOU!

THANK YOU!   THANK YOU!   THANK YOU!   THANK YOU!

THANK YOU!   THANK YOU!   THANK YOU!   THANK YOU!

THANK YOU!   THANK YOU!   THANK YOU!   THANK YOU!

THANK YOU!   THANK YOU!   THANK YOU!   THANK YOU!

THANK YOU!   THANK YOU!   THANK YOU!   THANK YOU!

THANK YOU!   THANK YOU!   THANK YOU!   THANK YOU!

THANK YOU!   THANK YOU!   THANK YOU!   THANK YOU!

THANK YOU!   THANK YOU!   THANK YOU!   THANK YOU!

THANK YOU!   THANK YOU!   THANK YOU!   THANK YOU!

THANK YOU!   THANK YOU!   THANK YOU!   THANK YOU!

THANK YOU! THANK YOU! THANK YOU! THANK YOU!

THANK YOU!	THANK YOU!	THANK YOU!	THANK YOU!
THANK YOU!	THANK YOU!	THANK YOU!	THANK YOU!
THANK YOU!	THANK YOU!	THANK YOU!	THANK YOU!
THANK YOU!	THANK YOU!	THANK YOU!	THANK YOU!
THANK YOU!	THANK YOU!	THANK YOU!	THANK YOU!
THANK YOU!	THANK YOU!	THANK YOU!	THANK YOU!
THANK YOU!	THANK YOU!	THANK YOU!	THANK YOU!
THANK YOU!	THANK YOU!	THANK YOU!	THANK YOU!
THANK YOU!	THANK YOU!	THANK YOU!	THANK YOU!
THANK YOU!	THANK YOU!	THANK YOU!	THANK YOU!
THANK YOU!	THANK YOU!	THANK YOU!	THANK YOU!
THANK YOU!	THANK YOU!	THANK YOU!	THANK YOU!
THANK YOU!	THANK YOU!	THANK YOU!	THANK YOU!
THANK YOU!	THANK YOU!	THANK YOU!	THANK YOU!
THANK YOU!	THANK YOU!	THANK YOU!	THANK YOU!

THANK YOU! THANK YOU! THANK YOU! THANK YOU!

THANK YOU!	THANK YOU!	THANK YOU!	THANK YOU!
THANK YOU!	THANK YOU!	THANK YOU!	THANK YOU!
THANK YOU!	THANK YOU!	THANK YOU!	THANK YOU!
THANK YOU!	THANK YOU!	THANK YOU!	THANK YOU!
THANK YOU!	THANK YOU!	THANK YOU!	THANK YOU!
THANK YOU!	THANK YOU!	THANK YOU!	THANK YOU!
THANK YOU!	THANK YOU!	THANK YOU!	THANK YOU!
THANK YOU!	THANK YOU!	THANK YOU!	THANK YOU!
THANK YOU!	THANK YOU!	THANK YOU!	THANK YOU!
THANK YOU!	THANK YOU!	THANK YOU!	THANK YOU!
THANK YOU!	THANK YOU!	THANK YOU!	THANK YOU!
THANK YOU!	THANK YOU!	THANK YOU!	THANK YOU!
THANK YOU!	THANK YOU!	THANK YOU!	THANK YOU!
THANK YOU!	THANK YOU!	THANK YOU!	THANK YOU!
THANK YOU!	THANK YOU!	THANK YOU!	THANK YOU!

THANK YOU! THANK YOU! THANK YOU! THANK YOU!

THANK YOU!	THANK YOU!	THANK YOU!	THANK YOU!
THANK YOU!	THANK YOU!	THANK YOU!	THANK YOU!
THANK YOU!	THANK YOU!	THANK YOU!	THANK YOU!
THANK YOU!	THANK YOU!	THANK YOU!	THANK YOU!
THANK YOU!	THANK YOU!	THANK YOU!	THANK YOU!
THANK YOU!	THANK YOU!	THANK YOU!	THANK YOU!
THANK YOU!	THANK YOU!	THANK YOU!	THANK YOU!
THANK YOU!	THANK YOU!	THANK YOU!	THANK YOU!
THANK YOU!	THANK YOU!	THANK YOU!	THANK YOU!
THANK YOU!	THANK YOU!	THANK YOU!	THANK YOU!
THANK YOU!	THANK YOU!	THANK YOU!	THANK YOU!
THANK YOU!	THANK YOU!	THANK YOU!	THANK YOU!
THANK YOU!	THANK YOU!	THANK YOU!	THANK YOU!
THANK YOU!	THANK YOU!	THANK YOU!	THANK YOU!
THANK YOU!	THANK YOU!	THANK YOU!	THANK YOU!
THANK YOU!	THANK YOU!	THANK YOU!	THANK YOU!

THANK YOU! THANK YOU! THANK YOU! THANK YOU!

THANK YOU! THANK YOU! THANK YOU! THANK YOU!

THANK YOU! THANK YOU! THANK YOU! THANK YOU!

THANK YOU! THANK YOU! THANK YOU! THANK YOU!

THANK YOU! THANK YOU! THANK YOU! THANK YOU!

THANK YOU! THANK YOU! THANK YOU! THANK YOU!

THANK YOU! THANK YOU! THANK YOU! THANK YOU!

THANK YOU! THANK YOU! THANK YOU! THANK YOU!

THANK YOU! THANK YOU! THANK YOU! THANK YOU!

THANK YOU! THANK YOU! THANK YOU! THANK YOU!

THANK YOU! THANK YOU! THANK YOU! THANK YOU!

THANK YOU! THANK YOU! THANK YOU! THANK YOU!

THANK YOU! THANK YOU! THANK YOU! THANK YOU!

THANK YOU! THANK YOU! THANK YOU! THANK YOU!

THANK YOU! THANK YOU! THANK YOU! THANK YOU!

THANK YOU! THANK YOU! THANK YOU! THANK YOU!

THANK YOU! THANK YOU! THANK YOU! THANK YOU!

THANK YOU!	THANK YOU!	THANK YOU!	THANK YOU!
THANK YOU!	THANK YOU!	THANK YOU!	THANK YOU!
THANK YOU!	THANK YOU!	THANK YOU!	THANK YOU!
THANK YOU!	THANK YOU!	THANK YOU!	THANK YOU!
THANK YOU!	THANK YOU!	THANK YOU!	THANK YOU!
THANK YOU!	THANK YOU!	THANK YOU!	THANK YOU!
THANK YOU!	THANK YOU!	THANK YOU!	THANK YOU!
THANK YOU!	THANK YOU!	THANK YOU!	THANK YOU!
THANK YOU!	THANK YOU!	THANK YOU!	THANK YOU!
THANK YOU!	THANK YOU!	THANK YOU!	THANK YOU!
THANK YOU!	THANK YOU!	THANK YOU!	THANK YOU!
THANK YOU!	THANK YOU!	THANK YOU!	THANK YOU!
THANK YOU!	THANK YOU!	THANK YOU!	THANK YOU!
THANK YOU!	THANK YOU!	THANK YOU!	THANK YOU!
THANK YOU!	THANK YOU!	THANK YOU!	THANK YOU!

THANK YOU! THANK YOU! THANK YOU! THANK YOU!

THANK YOU! THANK YOU! THANK YOU! THANK YOU!

THANK YOU! THANK YOU! THANK YOU! THANK YOU!

THANK YOU! THANK YOU! THANK YOU! THANK YOU!

THANK YOU! THANK YOU! THANK YOU! THANK YOU!

THANK YOU! THANK YOU! THANK YOU! THANK YOU!

THANK YOU! THANK YOU! THANK YOU! THANK YOU!

THANK YOU! THANK YOU! THANK YOU! THANK YOU!

THANK YOU! THANK YOU! THANK YOU! THANK YOU!

THANK YOU! THANK YOU! THANK YOU! THANK YOU!

THANK YOU! THANK YOU! THANK YOU! THANK YOU!

THANK YOU! THANK YOU! THANK YOU! THANK YOU!

THANK YOU! THANK YOU! THANK YOU! THANK YOU!

THANK YOU! THANK YOU! THANK YOU! THANK YOU!

THANK YOU! THANK YOU! THANK YOU! THANK YOU!

THANK YOU! THANK YOU! THANK YOU! THANK YOU!

THANK YOU! THANK YOU! THANK YOU! THANK YOU!

THANK YOU!	THANK YOU!	THANK YOU!	THANK YOU!
THANK YOU!	THANK YOU!	THANK YOU!	THANK YOU!
THANK YOU!	THANK YOU!	THANK YOU!	THANK YOU!
THANK YOU!	THANK YOU!	THANK YOU!	THANK YOU!
THANK YOU!	THANK YOU!	THANK YOU!	THANK YOU!
THANK YOU!	THANK YOU!	THANK YOU!	THANK YOU!
THANK YOU!	THANK YOU!	THANK YOU!	THANK YOU!
THANK YOU!	THANK YOU!	THANK YOU!	THANK YOU!
THANK YOU!	THANK YOU!	THANK YOU!	THANK YOU!
THANK YOU!	THANK YOU!	THANK YOU!	THANK YOU!
THANK YOU!	THANK YOU!	THANK YOU!	THANK YOU!
THANK YOU!	THANK YOU!	THANK YOU!	THANK YOU!
THANK YOU!	THANK YOU!	THANK YOU!	THANK YOU!
THANK YOU!	THANK YOU!	THANK YOU!	THANK YOU!
THANK YOU!	THANK YOU!	THANK YOU!	THANK YOU!

THANK YOU! THANK YOU! THANK YOU! THANK YOU!

THANK YOU!	THANK YOU!	THANK YOU!	THANK YOU!
THANK YOU!	THANK YOU!	THANK YOU!	THANK YOU!
THANK YOU!	THANK YOU!	THANK YOU!	THANK YOU!
THANK YOU!	THANK YOU!	THANK YOU!	THANK YOU!
THANK YOU!	THANK YOU!	THANK YOU!	THANK YOU!
THANK YOU!	THANK YOU!	THANK YOU!	THANK YOU!
THANK YOU!	THANK YOU!	THANK YOU!	THANK YOU!
THANK YOU!	THANK YOU!	THANK YOU!	THANK YOU!
THANK YOU!	THANK YOU!	THANK YOU!	THANK YOU!
THANK YOU!	THANK YOU!	THANK YOU!	THANK YOU!
THANK YOU!	THANK YOU!	THANK YOU!	THANK YOU!
THANK YOU!	THANK YOU!	THANK YOU!	THANK YOU!
THANK YOU!	THANK YOU!	THANK YOU!	THANK YOU!
THANK YOU!	THANK YOU!	THANK YOU!	THANK YOU!
THANK YOU!	THANK YOU!	THANK YOU!	THANK YOU!

THANK YOU! THANK YOU! THANK YOU! THANK YOU!

THANK YOU!	THANK YOU!	THANK YOU!	THANK YOU!
THANK YOU!	THANK YOU!	THANK YOU!	THANK YOU!
THANK YOU!	THANK YOU!	THANK YOU!	THANK YOU!
THANK YOU!	THANK YOU!	THANK YOU!	THANK YOU!
THANK YOU!	THANK YOU!	THANK YOU!	THANK YOU!
THANK YOU!	THANK YOU!	THANK YOU!	THANK YOU!
THANK YOU!	THANK YOU!	THANK YOU!	THANK YOU!
THANK YOU!	THANK YOU!	THANK YOU!	THANK YOU!
THANK YOU!	THANK YOU!	THANK YOU!	THANK YOU!
THANK YOU!	THANK YOU!	THANK YOU!	THANK YOU!
THANK YOU!	THANK YOU!	THANK YOU!	THANK YOU!
THANK YOU!	THANK YOU!	THANK YOU!	THANK YOU!
THANK YOU!	THANK YOU!	THANK YOU!	THANK YOU!
THANK YOU!	THANK YOU!	THANK YOU!	THANK YOU!
THANK YOU!	THANK YOU!	THANK YOU!	THANK YOU!

THANK YOU! THANK YOU! THANK YOU! THANK YOU!

THANK YOU!	THANK YOU!	THANK YOU!	THANK YOU!
THANK YOU!	THANK YOU!	THANK YOU!	THANK YOU!
THANK YOU!	THANK YOU!	THANK YOU!	THANK YOU!
THANK YOU!	THANK YOU!	THANK YOU!	THANK YOU!
THANK YOU!	THANK YOU!	THANK YOU!	THANK YOU!
THANK YOU!	THANK YOU!	THANK YOU!	THANK YOU!
THANK YOU!	THANK YOU!	THANK YOU!	THANK YOU!
THANK YOU!	THANK YOU!	THANK YOU!	THANK YOU!
THANK YOU!	THANK YOU!	THANK YOU!	THANK YOU!
THANK YOU!	THANK YOU!	THANK YOU!	THANK YOU!
THANK YOU!	THANK YOU!	THANK YOU!	THANK YOU!
THANK YOU!	THANK YOU!	THANK YOU!	THANK YOU!
THANK YOU!	THANK YOU!	THANK YOU!	THANK YOU!
THANK YOU!	THANK YOU!	THANK YOU!	THANK YOU!
THANK YOU!	THANK YOU!	THANK YOU!	THANK YOU!

THANK YOU! THANK YOU! THANK YOU! THANK YOU!

THANK YOU!	THANK YOU!	THANK YOU!	THANK YOU!
THANK YOU!	THANK YOU!	THANK YOU!	THANK YOU!
THANK YOU!	THANK YOU!	THANK YOU!	THANK YOU!
THANK YOU!	THANK YOU!	THANK YOU!	THANK YOU!
THANK YOU!	THANK YOU!	THANK YOU!	THANK YOU!
THANK YOU!	THANK YOU!	THANK YOU!	THANK YOU!
THANK YOU!	THANK YOU!	THANK YOU!	THANK YOU!
THANK YOU!	THANK YOU!	THANK YOU!	THANK YOU!
THANK YOU!	THANK YOU!	THANK YOU!	THANK YOU!
THANK YOU!	THANK YOU!	THANK YOU!	THANK YOU!
THANK YOU!	THANK YOU!	THANK YOU!	THANK YOU!
THANK YOU!	THANK YOU!	THANK YOU!	THANK YOU!
THANK YOU!	THANK YOU!	THANK YOU!	THANK YOU!
THANK YOU!	THANK YOU!	THANK YOU!	THANK YOU!
THANK YOU!	THANK YOU!	THANK YOU!	THANK YOU!

THANK YOU! THANK YOU! THANK YOU! THANK YOU!

THANK YOU! THANK YOU! THANK YOU! THANK YOU!

THANK YOU! THANK YOU! THANK YOU! THANK YOU!

THANK YOU! THANK YOU! THANK YOU! THANK YOU!

THANK YOU! THANK YOU! THANK YOU! THANK YOU!

THANK YOU! THANK YOU! THANK YOU! THANK YOU!

THANK YOU! THANK YOU! THANK YOU! THANK YOU!

THANK YOU! THANK YOU! THANK YOU! THANK YOU!

THANK YOU! THANK YOU! THANK YOU! THANK YOU!

THANK YOU! THANK YOU! THANK YOU! THANK YOU!

THANK YOU! THANK YOU! THANK YOU! THANK YOU!

THANK YOU! THANK YOU! THANK YOU! THANK YOU!

THANK YOU! THANK YOU! THANK YOU! THANK YOU!

THANK YOU! THANK YOU! THANK YOU! THANK YOU!

THANK YOU! THANK YOU! THANK YOU! THANK YOU!

THANK YOU! THANK YOU! THANK YOU! THANK YOU!

THANK YOU! THANK YOU! THANK YOU! THANK YOU!

THANK YOU! THANK YOU! THANK YOU! THANK YOU!

THANK YOU! THANK YOU! THANK YOU! THANK YOU!

THANK YOU! THANK YOU! THANK YOU! THANK YOU!

THANK YOU! THANK YOU! THANK YOU! THANK YOU!

THANK YOU! THANK YOU! THANK YOU! THANK YOU!

THANK YOU! THANK YOU! THANK YOU! THANK YOU!

THANK YOU! THANK YOU! THANK YOU! THANK YOU!

THANK YOU! THANK YOU! THANK YOU! THANK YOU!

THANK YOU! THANK YOU! THANK YOU! THANK YOU!

THANK YOU! THANK YOU! THANK YOU! THANK YOU!

THANK YOU! THANK YOU! THANK YOU! THANK YOU!

THANK YOU! THANK YOU! THANK YOU! THANK YOU!

THANK YOU! THANK YOU! THANK YOU! THANK YOU!

THANK YOU! THANK YOU! THANK YOU! THANK YOU!

THANK YOU! THANK YOU! THANK YOU! THANK YOU!

THANK YOU! THANK YOU! THANK YOU! THANK YOU!

THANK YOU!	THANK YOU!	THANK YOU!	THANK YOU!
THANK YOU!	THANK YOU!	THANK YOU!	THANK YOU!
THANK YOU!	THANK YOU!	THANK YOU!	THANK YOU!
THANK YOU!	THANK YOU!	THANK YOU!	THANK YOU!
THANK YOU!	THANK YOU!	THANK YOU!	THANK YOU!
THANK YOU!	THANK YOU!	THANK YOU!	THANK YOU!
THANK YOU!	THANK YOU!	THANK YOU!	THANK YOU!
THANK YOU!	THANK YOU!	THANK YOU!	THANK YOU!
THANK YOU!	THANK YOU!	THANK YOU!	THANK YOU!
THANK YOU!	THANK YOU!	THANK YOU!	THANK YOU!
THANK YOU!	THANK YOU!	THANK YOU!	THANK YOU!
THANK YOU!	THANK YOU!	THANK YOU!	THANK YOU!
THANK YOU!	THANK YOU!	THANK YOU!	THANK YOU!
THANK YOU!	THANK YOU!	THANK YOU!	THANK YOU!
THANK YOU!	THANK YOU!	THANK YOU!	THANK YOU!
THANK YOU!	THANK YOU!	THANK YOU!	THANK YOU!

THANK YOU! THANK YOU! THANK YOU! THANK YOU!

THANK YOU!	THANK YOU!	THANK YOU!	THANK YOU!
THANK YOU!	THANK YOU!	THANK YOU!	THANK YOU!
THANK YOU!	THANK YOU!	THANK YOU!	THANK YOU!
THANK YOU!	THANK YOU!	THANK YOU!	THANK YOU!
THANK YOU!	THANK YOU!	THANK YOU!	THANK YOU!
THANK YOU!	THANK YOU!	THANK YOU!	THANK YOU!
THANK YOU!	THANK YOU!	THANK YOU!	THANK YOU!
THANK YOU!	THANK YOU!	THANK YOU!	THANK YOU!
THANK YOU!	THANK YOU!	THANK YOU!	THANK YOU!
THANK YOU!	THANK YOU!	THANK YOU!	THANK YOU!
THANK YOU!	THANK YOU!	THANK YOU!	THANK YOU!
THANK YOU!	THANK YOU!	THANK YOU!	THANK YOU!
THANK YOU!	THANK YOU!	THANK YOU!	THANK YOU!
THANK YOU!	THANK YOU!	THANK YOU!	THANK YOU!
THANK YOU!	THANK YOU!	THANK YOU!	THANK YOU!

THANK YOU! THANK YOU! THANK YOU! THANK YOU!

THANK YOU!	THANK YOU!	THANK YOU!	THANK YOU!
THANK YOU!	THANK YOU!	THANK YOU!	THANK YOU!
THANK YOU!	THANK YOU!	THANK YOU!	THANK YOU!
THANK YOU!	THANK YOU!	THANK YOU!	THANK YOU!
THANK YOU!	THANK YOU!	THANK YOU!	THANK YOU!
THANK YOU!	THANK YOU!	THANK YOU!	THANK YOU!
THANK YOU!	THANK YOU!	THANK YOU!	THANK YOU!
THANK YOU!	THANK YOU!	THANK YOU!	THANK YOU!
THANK YOU!	THANK YOU!	THANK YOU!	THANK YOU!
THANK YOU!	THANK YOU!	THANK YOU!	THANK YOU!
THANK YOU!	THANK YOU!	THANK YOU!	THANK YOU!
THANK YOU!	THANK YOU!	THANK YOU!	THANK YOU!
THANK YOU!	THANK YOU!	THANK YOU!	THANK YOU!
THANK YOU!	THANK YOU!	THANK YOU!	THANK YOU!
THANK YOU!	THANK YOU!	THANK YOU!	THANK YOU!

THANK YOU! THANK YOU! THANK YOU! THANK YOU!

THANK YOU!	THANK YOU!	THANK YOU!	THANK YOU!
THANK YOU!	THANK YOU!	THANK YOU!	THANK YOU!
THANK YOU!	THANK YOU!	THANK YOU!	THANK YOU!
THANK YOU!	THANK YOU!	THANK YOU!	THANK YOU!
THANK YOU!	THANK YOU!	THANK YOU!	THANK YOU!
THANK YOU!	THANK YOU!	THANK YOU!	THANK YOU!
THANK YOU!	THANK YOU!	THANK YOU!	THANK YOU!
THANK YOU!	THANK YOU!	THANK YOU!	THANK YOU!
THANK YOU!	THANK YOU!	THANK YOU!	THANK YOU!
THANK YOU!	THANK YOU!	THANK YOU!	THANK YOU!
THANK YOU!	THANK YOU!	THANK YOU!	THANK YOU!
THANK YOU!	THANK YOU!	THANK YOU!	THANK YOU!
THANK YOU!	THANK YOU!	THANK YOU!	THANK YOU!
THANK YOU!	THANK YOU!	THANK YOU!	THANK YOU!
THANK YOU!	THANK YOU!	THANK YOU!	THANK YOU!

THANK YOU! THANK YOU! THANK YOU! THANK YOU!

THANK YOU! THANK YOU! THANK YOU! THANK YOU!

THANK YOU! THANK YOU! THANK YOU! THANK YOU!

THANK YOU! THANK YOU! THANK YOU! THANK YOU!

THANK YOU! THANK YOU! THANK YOU! THANK YOU!

THANK YOU! THANK YOU! THANK YOU! THANK YOU!

THANK YOU! THANK YOU! THANK YOU! THANK YOU!

THANK YOU! THANK YOU! THANK YOU! THANK YOU!

THANK YOU! THANK YOU! THANK YOU! THANK YOU!

THANK YOU! THANK YOU! THANK YOU! THANK YOU!

THANK YOU! THANK YOU! THANK YOU! THANK YOU!

THANK YOU! THANK YOU! THANK YOU! THANK YOU!

THANK YOU! THANK YOU! THANK YOU! THANK YOU!

THANK YOU! THANK YOU! THANK YOU! THANK YOU!

THANK YOU! THANK YOU! THANK YOU! THANK YOU!

THANK YOU! THANK YOU! THANK YOU! THANK YOU!

THANK YOU! THANK YOU! THANK YOU! THANK YOU!

THANK YOU!	THANK YOU!	THANK YOU!	THANK YOU!
THANK YOU!	THANK YOU!	THANK YOU!	THANK YOU!
THANK YOU!	THANK YOU!	THANK YOU!	THANK YOU!
THANK YOU!	THANK YOU!	THANK YOU!	THANK YOU!
THANK YOU!	THANK YOU!	THANK YOU!	THANK YOU!
THANK YOU!	THANK YOU!	THANK YOU!	THANK YOU!
THANK YOU!	THANK YOU!	THANK YOU!	THANK YOU!
THANK YOU!	THANK YOU!	THANK YOU!	THANK YOU!
THANK YOU!	THANK YOU!	THANK YOU!	THANK YOU!
THANK YOU!	THANK YOU!	THANK YOU!	THANK YOU!
THANK YOU!	THANK YOU!	THANK YOU!	THANK YOU!
THANK YOU!	THANK YOU!	THANK YOU!	THANK YOU!
THANK YOU!	THANK YOU!	THANK YOU!	THANK YOU!
THANK YOU!	THANK YOU!	THANK YOU!	THANK YOU!
THANK YOU!	THANK YOU!	THANK YOU!	THANK YOU!

THANK YOU! THANK YOU! THANK YOU! THANK YOU!

THANK YOU!   THANK YOU!   THANK YOU!   THANK YOU!

THANK YOU!   THANK YOU!   THANK YOU!   THANK YOU!

THANK YOU!   THANK YOU!   THANK YOU!   THANK YOU!

THANK YOU!   THANK YOU!   THANK YOU!   THANK YOU!

THANK YOU!   THANK YOU!   THANK YOU!   THANK YOU!

THANK YOU!   THANK YOU!   THANK YOU!   THANK YOU!

THANK YOU!   THANK YOU!   THANK YOU!   THANK YOU!

THANK YOU!   THANK YOU!   THANK YOU!   THANK YOU!

THANK YOU!   THANK YOU!   THANK YOU!   THANK YOU!

THANK YOU!   THANK YOU!   THANK YOU!   THANK YOU!

THANK YOU!   THANK YOU!   THANK YOU!   THANK YOU!

THANK YOU!   THANK YOU!   THANK YOU!   THANK YOU!

THANK YOU!   THANK YOU!   THANK YOU!   THANK YOU!

THANK YOU!   THANK YOU!   THANK YOU!   THANK YOU!

THANK YOU!   THANK YOU!   THANK YOU!   THANK YOU!

THANK YOU! THANK YOU! THANK YOU! THANK YOU!

THANK YOU!   THANK YOU!   THANK YOU!   THANK YOU!

THANK YOU!   THANK YOU!   THANK YOU!   THANK YOU!

THANK YOU!   THANK YOU!   THANK YOU!   THANK YOU!

THANK YOU!   THANK YOU!   THANK YOU!   THANK YOU!

THANK YOU!   THANK YOU!   THANK YOU!   THANK YOU!

THANK YOU!   THANK YOU!   THANK YOU!   THANK YOU!

THANK YOU!   THANK YOU!   THANK YOU!   THANK YOU!

THANK YOU!   THANK YOU!   THANK YOU!   THANK YOU!

THANK YOU!   THANK YOU!   THANK YOU!   THANK YOU!

THANK YOU!   THANK YOU!   THANK YOU!   THANK YOU!

THANK YOU!   THANK YOU!   THANK YOU!   THANK YOU!

THANK YOU!   THANK YOU!   THANK YOU!   THANK YOU!

THANK YOU!   THANK YOU!   THANK YOU!   THANK YOU!

THANK YOU!   THANK YOU!   THANK YOU!   THANK YOU!

THANK YOU!   THANK YOU!   THANK YOU!   THANK YOU!

THANK YOU! THANK YOU! THANK YOU! THANK YOU!

THANK YOU!	THANK YOU!	THANK YOU!	THANK YOU!
THANK YOU!	THANK YOU!	THANK YOU!	THANK YOU!
THANK YOU!	THANK YOU!	THANK YOU!	THANK YOU!
THANK YOU!	THANK YOU!	THANK YOU!	THANK YOU!
THANK YOU!	THANK YOU!	THANK YOU!	THANK YOU!
THANK YOU!	THANK YOU!	THANK YOU!	THANK YOU!
THANK YOU!	THANK YOU!	THANK YOU!	THANK YOU!
THANK YOU!	THANK YOU!	THANK YOU!	THANK YOU!
THANK YOU!	THANK YOU!	THANK YOU!	THANK YOU!
THANK YOU!	THANK YOU!	THANK YOU!	THANK YOU!
THANK YOU!	THANK YOU!	THANK YOU!	THANK YOU!
THANK YOU!	THANK YOU!	THANK YOU!	THANK YOU!
THANK YOU!	THANK YOU!	THANK YOU!	THANK YOU!
THANK YOU!	THANK YOU!	THANK YOU!	THANK YOU!
THANK YOU!	THANK YOU!	THANK YOU!	THANK YOU!

THANK YOU! THANK YOU! THANK YOU! THANK YOU!

THANK YOU!	THANK YOU!	THANK YOU!	THANK YOU!
THANK YOU!	THANK YOU!	THANK YOU!	THANK YOU!
THANK YOU!	THANK YOU!	THANK YOU!	THANK YOU!
THANK YOU!	THANK YOU!	THANK YOU!	THANK YOU!
THANK YOU!	THANK YOU!	THANK YOU!	THANK YOU!
THANK YOU!	THANK YOU!	THANK YOU!	THANK YOU!
THANK YOU!	THANK YOU!	THANK YOU!	THANK YOU!
THANK YOU!	THANK YOU!	THANK YOU!	THANK YOU!
THANK YOU!	THANK YOU!	THANK YOU!	THANK YOU!
THANK YOU!	THANK YOU!	THANK YOU!	THANK YOU!
THANK YOU!	THANK YOU!	THANK YOU!	THANK YOU!
THANK YOU!	THANK YOU!	THANK YOU!	THANK YOU!
THANK YOU!	THANK YOU!	THANK YOU!	THANK YOU!
THANK YOU!	THANK YOU!	THANK YOU!	THANK YOU!
THANK YOU!	THANK YOU!	THANK YOU!	THANK YOU!

THANK YOU! THANK YOU! THANK YOU! THANK YOU!

THANK YOU!   THANK YOU!   THANK YOU!   THANK YOU!

THANK YOU!   THANK YOU!   THANK YOU!   THANK YOU!

THANK YOU!   THANK YOU!   THANK YOU!   THANK YOU!

THANK YOU!   THANK YOU!   THANK YOU!   THANK YOU!

THANK YOU!   THANK YOU!   THANK YOU!   THANK YOU!

THANK YOU!   THANK YOU!   THANK YOU!   THANK YOU!

THANK YOU!   THANK YOU!   THANK YOU!   THANK YOU!

THANK YOU!   THANK YOU!   THANK YOU!   THANK YOU!

THANK YOU!   THANK YOU!   THANK YOU!   THANK YOU!

THANK YOU!   THANK YOU!   THANK YOU!   THANK YOU!

THANK YOU!   THANK YOU!   THANK YOU!   THANK YOU!

THANK YOU!   THANK YOU!   THANK YOU!   THANK YOU!

THANK YOU!   THANK YOU!   THANK YOU!   THANK YOU!

THANK YOU!   THANK YOU!   THANK YOU!   THANK YOU!

THANK YOU!   THANK YOU!   THANK YOU!   THANK YOU!

THANK YOU! THANK YOU! THANK YOU! THANK YOU!

THANK YOU! THANK YOU! THANK YOU! THANK YOU!

THANK YOU! THANK YOU! THANK YOU! THANK YOU!

THANK YOU! THANK YOU! THANK YOU! THANK YOU!

THANK YOU! THANK YOU! THANK YOU! THANK YOU!

THANK YOU! THANK YOU! THANK YOU! THANK YOU!

THANK YOU! THANK YOU! THANK YOU! THANK YOU!

THANK YOU! THANK YOU! THANK YOU! THANK YOU!

THANK YOU! THANK YOU! THANK YOU! THANK YOU!

THANK YOU! THANK YOU! THANK YOU! THANK YOU!

THANK YOU! THANK YOU! THANK YOU! THANK YOU!

THANK YOU! THANK YOU! THANK YOU! THANK YOU!

THANK YOU! THANK YOU! THANK YOU! THANK YOU!

THANK YOU! THANK YOU! THANK YOU! THANK YOU!

THANK YOU! THANK YOU! THANK YOU! THANK YOU!

THANK YOU! THANK YOU! THANK YOU! THANK YOU!

THANK YOU!   THANK YOU!   THANK YOU!   THANK YOU!

THANK YOU!   THANK YOU!   THANK YOU!   THANK YOU!

THANK YOU!   THANK YOU!   THANK YOU!   THANK YOU!

THANK YOU!   THANK YOU!   THANK YOU!   THANK YOU!

THANK YOU!   THANK YOU!   THANK YOU!   THANK YOU!

THANK YOU!   THANK YOU!   THANK YOU!   THANK YOU!

THANK YOU!   THANK YOU!   THANK YOU!   THANK YOU!

THANK YOU!   THANK YOU!   THANK YOU!   THANK YOU!

THANK YOU!   THANK YOU!   THANK YOU!   THANK YOU!

THANK YOU!   THANK YOU!   THANK YOU!   THANK YOU!

THANK YOU!   THANK YOU!   THANK YOU!   THANK YOU!

THANK YOU!   THANK YOU!   THANK YOU!   THANK YOU!

THANK YOU!   THANK YOU!   THANK YOU!   THANK YOU!

THANK YOU!   THANK YOU!   THANK YOU!   THANK YOU!

THANK YOU!   THANK YOU!   THANK YOU!   THANK YOU!

THANK YOU! THANK YOU! THANK YOU! THANK YOU!

THANK YOU! THANK YOU! THANK YOU! THANK YOU!

THANK YOU! THANK YOU! THANK YOU! THANK YOU!

THANK YOU! THANK YOU! THANK YOU! THANK YOU!

THANK YOU! THANK YOU! THANK YOU! THANK YOU!

THANK YOU! THANK YOU! THANK YOU! THANK YOU!

THANK YOU! THANK YOU! THANK YOU! THANK YOU!

THANK YOU! THANK YOU! THANK YOU! THANK YOU!

THANK YOU! THANK YOU! THANK YOU! THANK YOU!

THANK YOU! THANK YOU! THANK YOU! THANK YOU!

THANK YOU! THANK YOU! THANK YOU! THANK YOU!

THANK YOU! THANK YOU! THANK YOU! THANK YOU!

THANK YOU! THANK YOU! THANK YOU! THANK YOU!

THANK YOU! THANK YOU! THANK YOU! THANK YOU!

THANK YOU! THANK YOU! THANK YOU! THANK YOU!

THANK YOU! THANK YOU! THANK YOU! THANK YOU!

THANK YOU! THANK YOU! THANK YOU! THANK YOU!

THANK YOU!   THANK YOU!   THANK YOU!   THANK YOU!

THANK YOU!   THANK YOU!   THANK YOU!   THANK YOU!

THANK YOU!   THANK YOU!   THANK YOU!   THANK YOU!

THANK YOU!   THANK YOU!   THANK YOU!   THANK YOU!

THANK YOU!   THANK YOU!   THANK YOU!   THANK YOU!

THANK YOU!   THANK YOU!   THANK YOU!   THANK YOU!

THANK YOU!   THANK YOU!   THANK YOU!   THANK YOU!

THANK YOU!   THANK YOU!   THANK YOU!   THANK YOU!

THANK YOU!   THANK YOU!   THANK YOU!   THANK YOU!

THANK YOU!   THANK YOU!   THANK YOU!   THANK YOU!

THANK YOU!   THANK YOU!   THANK YOU!   THANK YOU!

THANK YOU!   THANK YOU!   THANK YOU!   THANK YOU!

THANK YOU!   THANK YOU!   THANK YOU!   THANK YOU!

THANK YOU!   THANK YOU!   THANK YOU!   THANK YOU!

THANK YOU!   THANK YOU!   THANK YOU!   THANK YOU!

THANK YOU! THANK YOU! THANK YOU! THANK YOU!

THANK YOU!	THANK YOU!	THANK YOU!	THANK YOU!
THANK YOU!	THANK YOU!	THANK YOU!	THANK YOU!
THANK YOU!	THANK YOU!	THANK YOU!	THANK YOU!
THANK YOU!	THANK YOU!	THANK YOU!	THANK YOU!
THANK YOU!	THANK YOU!	THANK YOU!	THANK YOU!
THANK YOU!	THANK YOU!	THANK YOU!	THANK YOU!
THANK YOU!	THANK YOU!	THANK YOU!	THANK YOU!
THANK YOU!	THANK YOU!	THANK YOU!	THANK YOU!
THANK YOU!	THANK YOU!	THANK YOU!	THANK YOU!
THANK YOU!	THANK YOU!	THANK YOU!	THANK YOU!
THANK YOU!	THANK YOU!	THANK YOU!	THANK YOU!
THANK YOU!	THANK YOU!	THANK YOU!	THANK YOU!
THANK YOU!	THANK YOU!	THANK YOU!	THANK YOU!
THANK YOU!	THANK YOU!	THANK YOU!	THANK YOU!
THANK YOU!	THANK YOU!	THANK YOU!	THANK YOU!

THANK YOU! THANK YOU! THANK YOU! THANK YOU!

THANK YOU!	THANK YOU!	THANK YOU!	THANK YOU!
THANK YOU!	THANK YOU!	THANK YOU!	THANK YOU!
THANK YOU!	THANK YOU!	THANK YOU!	THANK YOU!
THANK YOU!	THANK YOU!	THANK YOU!	THANK YOU!
THANK YOU!	THANK YOU!	THANK YOU!	THANK YOU!
THANK YOU!	THANK YOU!	THANK YOU!	THANK YOU!
THANK YOU!	THANK YOU!	THANK YOU!	THANK YOU!
THANK YOU!	THANK YOU!	THANK YOU!	THANK YOU!
THANK YOU!	THANK YOU!	THANK YOU!	THANK YOU!
THANK YOU!	THANK YOU!	THANK YOU!	THANK YOU!
THANK YOU!	THANK YOU!	THANK YOU!	THANK YOU!
THANK YOU!	THANK YOU!	THANK YOU!	THANK YOU!
THANK YOU!	THANK YOU!	THANK YOU!	THANK YOU!
THANK YOU!	THANK YOU!	THANK YOU!	THANK YOU!
THANK YOU!	THANK YOU!	THANK YOU!	THANK YOU!

THANK YOU! THANK YOU! THANK YOU! THANK YOU!

THANK YOU! THANK YOU! THANK YOU! THANK YOU!

THANK YOU! THANK YOU! THANK YOU! THANK YOU!

THANK YOU! THANK YOU! THANK YOU! THANK YOU!

THANK YOU! THANK YOU! THANK YOU! THANK YOU!

THANK YOU! THANK YOU! THANK YOU! THANK YOU!

THANK YOU! THANK YOU! THANK YOU! THANK YOU!

THANK YOU! THANK YOU! THANK YOU! THANK YOU!

THANK YOU! THANK YOU! THANK YOU! THANK YOU!

THANK YOU! THANK YOU! THANK YOU! THANK YOU!

THANK YOU! THANK YOU! THANK YOU! THANK YOU!

THANK YOU! THANK YOU! THANK YOU! THANK YOU!

THANK YOU! THANK YOU! THANK YOU! THANK YOU!

THANK YOU! THANK YOU! THANK YOU! THANK YOU!

THANK YOU! THANK YOU! THANK YOU! THANK YOU!

THANK YOU! THANK YOU! THANK YOU! THANK YOU!

THANK YOU! THANK YOU! THANK YOU! THANK YOU!

THANK YOU!   THANK YOU!   THANK YOU!   THANK YOU!

THANK YOU!   THANK YOU!   THANK YOU!   THANK YOU!

THANK YOU!   THANK YOU!   THANK YOU!   THANK YOU!

THANK YOU!   THANK YOU!   THANK YOU!   THANK YOU!

THANK YOU!   THANK YOU!   THANK YOU!   THANK YOU!

THANK YOU!   THANK YOU!   THANK YOU!   THANK YOU!

THANK YOU!   THANK YOU!   THANK YOU!   THANK YOU!

THANK YOU!   THANK YOU!   THANK YOU!   THANK YOU!

THANK YOU!   THANK YOU!   THANK YOU!   THANK YOU!

THANK YOU!   THANK YOU!   THANK YOU!   THANK YOU!

THANK YOU!   THANK YOU!   THANK YOU!   THANK YOU!

THANK YOU!   THANK YOU!   THANK YOU!   THANK YOU!

THANK YOU!   THANK YOU!   THANK YOU!   THANK YOU!

THANK YOU!   THANK YOU!   THANK YOU!   THANK YOU!

THANK YOU!   THANK YOU!   THANK YOU!   THANK YOU!

THANK YOU! THANK YOU! THANK YOU! THANK YOU!

THANK YOU! THANK YOU! THANK YOU! THANK YOU!

THANK YOU! THANK YOU! THANK YOU! THANK YOU!

THANK YOU! THANK YOU! THANK YOU! THANK YOU!

THANK YOU! THANK YOU! THANK YOU! THANK YOU!

THANK YOU! THANK YOU! THANK YOU! THANK YOU!

THANK YOU! THANK YOU! THANK YOU! THANK YOU!

THANK YOU! THANK YOU! THANK YOU! THANK YOU!

THANK YOU! THANK YOU! THANK YOU! THANK YOU!

THANK YOU! THANK YOU! THANK YOU! THANK YOU!

THANK YOU! THANK YOU! THANK YOU! THANK YOU!

THANK YOU! THANK YOU! THANK YOU! THANK YOU!

THANK YOU! THANK YOU! THANK YOU! THANK YOU!

THANK YOU! THANK YOU! THANK YOU! THANK YOU!

THANK YOU! THANK YOU! THANK YOU! THANK YOU!

THANK YOU! THANK YOU! THANK YOU! THANK YOU!

THANK YOU! THANK YOU! THANK YOU! THANK YOU!

THANK YOU! THANK YOU! THANK YOU! THANK YOU!

THANK YOU! THANK YOU! THANK YOU! THANK YOU!

THANK YOU! THANK YOU! THANK YOU! THANK YOU!

THANK YOU! THANK YOU! THANK YOU! THANK YOU!

THANK YOU! THANK YOU! THANK YOU! THANK YOU!

THANK YOU! THANK YOU! THANK YOU! THANK YOU!

THANK YOU! THANK YOU! THANK YOU! THANK YOU!

THANK YOU! THANK YOU! THANK YOU! THANK YOU!

THANK YOU! THANK YOU! THANK YOU! THANK YOU!

THANK YOU! THANK YOU! THANK YOU! THANK YOU!

THANK YOU! THANK YOU! THANK YOU! THANK YOU!

THANK YOU! THANK YOU! THANK YOU! THANK YOU!

THANK YOU! THANK YOU! THANK YOU! THANK YOU!

THANK YOU! THANK YOU! THANK YOU! THANK YOU!

THANK YOU! THANK YOU! THANK YOU! THANK YOU!

THANK YOU! THANK YOU! THANK YOU! THANK YOU!

THANK YOU!	THANK YOU!	THANK YOU!	THANK YOU!
THANK YOU!	THANK YOU!	THANK YOU!	THANK YOU!
THANK YOU!	THANK YOU!	THANK YOU!	THANK YOU!
THANK YOU!	THANK YOU!	THANK YOU!	THANK YOU!
THANK YOU!	THANK YOU!	THANK YOU!	THANK YOU!
THANK YOU!	THANK YOU!	THANK YOU!	THANK YOU!
THANK YOU!	THANK YOU!	THANK YOU!	THANK YOU!
THANK YOU!	THANK YOU!	THANK YOU!	THANK YOU!
THANK YOU!	THANK YOU!	THANK YOU!	THANK YOU!
THANK YOU!	THANK YOU!	THANK YOU!	THANK YOU!
THANK YOU!	THANK YOU!	THANK YOU!	THANK YOU!
THANK YOU!	THANK YOU!	THANK YOU!	THANK YOU!
THANK YOU!	THANK YOU!	THANK YOU!	THANK YOU!
THANK YOU!	THANK YOU!	THANK YOU!	THANK YOU!
THANK YOU!	THANK YOU!	THANK YOU!	THANK YOU!

THANK YOU! THANK YOU! THANK YOU! THANK YOU!

THANK YOU! THANK YOU! THANK YOU! THANK YOU!

THANK YOU! THANK YOU! THANK YOU! THANK YOU!

THANK YOU! THANK YOU! THANK YOU! THANK YOU!

THANK YOU! THANK YOU! THANK YOU! THANK YOU!

THANK YOU! THANK YOU! THANK YOU! THANK YOU!

THANK YOU! THANK YOU! THANK YOU! THANK YOU!

THANK YOU! THANK YOU! THANK YOU! THANK YOU!

THANK YOU! THANK YOU! THANK YOU! THANK YOU!

THANK YOU! THANK YOU! THANK YOU! THANK YOU!

THANK YOU! THANK YOU! THANK YOU! THANK YOU!

THANK YOU! THANK YOU! THANK YOU! THANK YOU!

THANK YOU! THANK YOU! THANK YOU! THANK YOU!

THANK YOU! THANK YOU! THANK YOU! THANK YOU!

THANK YOU! THANK YOU! THANK YOU! THANK YOU!

THANK YOU! THANK YOU! THANK YOU! THANK YOU!

THANK YOU! THANK YOU! THANK YOU! THANK YOU!

THANK YOU! THANK YOU! THANK YOU! THANK YOU!

THANK YOU!   THANK YOU!   THANK YOU!   THANK YOU!

THANK YOU!   THANK YOU!   THANK YOU!   THANK YOU!

THANK YOU!   THANK YOU!   THANK YOU!   THANK YOU!

THANK YOU!   THANK YOU!   THANK YOU!   THANK YOU!

THANK YOU!   THANK YOU!   THANK YOU!   THANK YOU!

THANK YOU!   THANK YOU!   THANK YOU!   THANK YOU!

THANK YOU!   THANK YOU!   THANK YOU!   THANK YOU!

THANK YOU!   THANK YOU!   THANK YOU!   THANK YOU!

THANK YOU!   THANK YOU!   THANK YOU!   THANK YOU!

THANK YOU!   THANK YOU!   THANK YOU!   THANK YOU!

THANK YOU!   THANK YOU!   THANK YOU!   THANK YOU!

THANK YOU!   THANK YOU!   THANK YOU!   THANK YOU!

THANK YOU!   THANK YOU!   THANK YOU!   THANK YOU!

THANK YOU!   THANK YOU!   THANK YOU!   THANK YOU!

THANK YOU!   THANK YOU!   THANK YOU!   THANK YOU!

THANK YOU! THANK YOU! THANK YOU! THANK YOU!

THANK YOU!   THANK YOU!   THANK YOU!   THANK YOU!

THANK YOU!   THANK YOU!   THANK YOU!   THANK YOU!

THANK YOU!   THANK YOU!   THANK YOU!   THANK YOU!

THANK YOU!   THANK YOU!   THANK YOU!   THANK YOU!

THANK YOU!   THANK YOU!   THANK YOU!   THANK YOU!

THANK YOU!   THANK YOU!   THANK YOU!   THANK YOU!

THANK YOU!   THANK YOU!   THANK YOU!   THANK YOU!

THANK YOU!   THANK YOU!   THANK YOU!   THANK YOU!

THANK YOU!   THANK YOU!   THANK YOU!   THANK YOU!

THANK YOU!   THANK YOU!   THANK YOU!   THANK YOU!

THANK YOU!   THANK YOU!   THANK YOU!   THANK YOU!

THANK YOU!   THANK YOU!   THANK YOU!   THANK YOU!

THANK YOU!   THANK YOU!   THANK YOU!   THANK YOU!

THANK YOU!   THANK YOU!   THANK YOU!   THANK YOU!

THANK YOU!   THANK YOU!   THANK YOU!   THANK YOU!

THANK YOU! THANK YOU! THANK YOU! THANK YOU!

THANK YOU!   THANK YOU!   THANK YOU!   THANK YOU!

THANK YOU!   THANK YOU!   THANK YOU!   THANK YOU!

THANK YOU!   THANK YOU!   THANK YOU!   THANK YOU!

THANK YOU!   THANK YOU!   THANK YOU!   THANK YOU!

THANK YOU!   THANK YOU!   THANK YOU!   THANK YOU!

THANK YOU!   THANK YOU!   THANK YOU!   THANK YOU!

THANK YOU!   THANK YOU!   THANK YOU!   THANK YOU!

THANK YOU!   THANK YOU!   THANK YOU!   THANK YOU!

THANK YOU!   THANK YOU!   THANK YOU!   THANK YOU!

THANK YOU!   THANK YOU!   THANK YOU!   THANK YOU!

THANK YOU!   THANK YOU!   THANK YOU!   THANK YOU!

THANK YOU!   THANK YOU!   THANK YOU!   THANK YOU!

THANK YOU!   THANK YOU!   THANK YOU!   THANK YOU!

THANK YOU!   THANK YOU!   THANK YOU!   THANK YOU!

THANK YOU!   THANK YOU!   THANK YOU!   THANK YOU!

THANK YOU!   THANK YOU!   THANK YOU!   THANK YOU!

THANK YOU! THANK YOU! THANK YOU! THANK YOU!

THANK YOU! THANK YOU! THANK YOU! THANK YOU!

THANK YOU! THANK YOU! THANK YOU! THANK YOU!

THANK YOU! THANK YOU! THANK YOU! THANK YOU!

THANK YOU! THANK YOU! THANK YOU! THANK YOU!

THANK YOU! THANK YOU! THANK YOU! THANK YOU!

THANK YOU! THANK YOU! THANK YOU! THANK YOU!

THANK YOU! THANK YOU! THANK YOU! THANK YOU!

THANK YOU! THANK YOU! THANK YOU! THANK YOU!

THANK YOU! THANK YOU! THANK YOU! THANK YOU!

THANK YOU! THANK YOU! THANK YOU! THANK YOU!

THANK YOU! THANK YOU! THANK YOU! THANK YOU!

THANK YOU! THANK YOU! THANK YOU! THANK YOU!

THANK YOU! THANK YOU! THANK YOU! THANK YOU!

THANK YOU! THANK YOU! THANK YOU! THANK YOU!

THANK YOU! THANK YOU! THANK YOU! THANK YOU!

THANK YOU!	THANK YOU!	THANK YOU!	THANK YOU!
THANK YOU!	THANK YOU!	THANK YOU!	THANK YOU!
THANK YOU!	THANK YOU!	THANK YOU!	THANK YOU!
THANK YOU!	THANK YOU!	THANK YOU!	THANK YOU!
THANK YOU!	THANK YOU!	THANK YOU!	THANK YOU!
THANK YOU!	THANK YOU!	THANK YOU!	THANK YOU!
THANK YOU!	THANK YOU!	THANK YOU!	THANK YOU!
THANK YOU!	THANK YOU!	THANK YOU!	THANK YOU!
THANK YOU!	THANK YOU!	THANK YOU!	THANK YOU!
THANK YOU!	THANK YOU!	THANK YOU!	THANK YOU!
THANK YOU!	THANK YOU!	THANK YOU!	THANK YOU!
THANK YOU!	THANK YOU!	THANK YOU!	THANK YOU!
THANK YOU!	THANK YOU!	THANK YOU!	THANK YOU!
THANK YOU!	THANK YOU!	THANK YOU!	THANK YOU!
THANK YOU!	THANK YOU!	THANK YOU!	THANK YOU!

THANK YOU! THANK YOU! THANK YOU! THANK YOU!

THANK YOU! THANK YOU! THANK YOU! THANK YOU!

THANK YOU! THANK YOU! THANK YOU! THANK YOU!

THANK YOU! THANK YOU! THANK YOU! THANK YOU!

THANK YOU! THANK YOU! THANK YOU! THANK YOU!

THANK YOU! THANK YOU! THANK YOU! THANK YOU!

THANK YOU! THANK YOU! THANK YOU! THANK YOU!

THANK YOU! THANK YOU! THANK YOU! THANK YOU!

THANK YOU! THANK YOU! THANK YOU! THANK YOU!

THANK YOU! THANK YOU! THANK YOU! THANK YOU!

THANK YOU! THANK YOU! THANK YOU! THANK YOU!

THANK YOU! THANK YOU! THANK YOU! THANK YOU!

THANK YOU! THANK YOU! THANK YOU! THANK YOU!

THANK YOU! THANK YOU! THANK YOU! THANK YOU!

THANK YOU! THANK YOU! THANK YOU! THANK YOU!

THANK YOU! THANK YOU! THANK YOU! THANK YOU!

THANK YOU! THANK YOU! THANK YOU! THANK YOU!

THANK YOU! THANK YOU! THANK YOU! THANK YOU!

THANK YOU! THANK YOU! THANK YOU! THANK YOU!

THANK YOU! THANK YOU! THANK YOU! THANK YOU!

THANK YOU! THANK YOU! THANK YOU! THANK YOU!

THANK YOU! THANK YOU! THANK YOU! THANK YOU!

THANK YOU! THANK YOU! THANK YOU! THANK YOU!

THANK YOU! THANK YOU! THANK YOU! THANK YOU!

THANK YOU! THANK YOU! THANK YOU! THANK YOU!

THANK YOU! THANK YOU! THANK YOU! THANK YOU!

THANK YOU! THANK YOU! THANK YOU! THANK YOU!

THANK YOU! THANK YOU! THANK YOU! THANK YOU!

THANK YOU! THANK YOU! THANK YOU! THANK YOU!

THANK YOU! THANK YOU! THANK YOU! THANK YOU!

THANK YOU! THANK YOU! THANK YOU! THANK YOU!